MARY SLESSOR

HEROES OF THE CROSS

DAVID LIVINGSTONE

MARY SLESSOR

JOHN WESLEY

WILFRED GRENFELL

MARY SLESSOR

MARSHALLS

Marshall Morgan & Scott
31 Beggarwood Lane, Basingstoke, Hants

Copyright © Marshall Morgan & Scott 1982

First published by Oliphants Ltd 1953
First issued in paperback in Lakeland 1961

This edition 1982
Impression number 10 9 8 7 6 5 4 3 2

ISBN: 0 551 00943 8

Printed in Great Britain by Richard Clay (The Chaucer Press) Ltd,
Bungay, Suffolk

CONTENTS

A SCOTTISH LASSIE'S VISION

HISTORY books tell us that the year 1848 was a very important one. It was a year of what they call Revolutions, and that means that certain men, angry at the conditions in which they lived, were fighting to overthrow those whom they considered to be bad and cruel rulers. Now the Christian religion is very much like a revolution, for it means the overthrow of one ruler, Satan, and the enthronement of Christ as Ruler and Lord. That kind of revolution is the only kind that does lasting good.

It so happens in that very year of 1848 there was born one who was destined to lead a revolution in a part of Africa where the powers of evil had held sway without interference for many centuries. Her name was Mary Mitchell Slessor and she was born on December 2nd in the great Scottish city of Aberdeen. She was the second of a family of seven children. Her mother was a good woman, devoted to the best interests of her children, but her father was the cause of much unhappiness in their home. He was a shoemaker by trade, but he spent much of his earnings on drink and did not care whether his family had enough to eat and to wear. Mrs. Slessor, who had been brought up in a comfortable home, had to go out to work herself in order to obtain the necessities of life for herself and her children. Sometimes the family would go without food themselves to provide a meal for their father, only to see him return home under the influence of drink and throw his dinner on the fire. Often Mary and her brothers and sisters would go outside and walk about in the streets until their father became sober.

The growing children were taught by their mother and at Sunday School the wonderful stories of the Bible, and early in life they came to know the Lord Jesus as their Saviour and Friend. They had heard thrilling stories of men and women who had gone out from Scotland to Africa to teach the way of Christ to millions of negroes whom had never heard of Him. They heard of terrible customs, like the killing of innocent babies and the slaughter of slaves. Robert, the eldest, already longed to become a missionary and he promised Mary that when his ambition was fulfilled he would take her into the pulpit with him. Mary herself used to set her dolls around her and pretend that they were negro boys and girls; she then told them the things she had learned at Sunday School, especially the "old, old story of Jesus and His love."

But not all her childhood was spent as seriously as that. Full of life and fun herself, she was often leading others in mischievous pranks. She loved to knock on folks' doors and then run away and hide round the corner while they answered the doors to find no one there. She was not a pretty girl. She was rather plain, with red, curly hair.

We would probably have called her a tomboy. She used to say that she had been a "wild lassie."

When Mary was about eleven years old the Slessor family moved to Dundee.

If you look at a map of Scotland, you will find Dundee on the east coast, a little way north of Edinburgh and some way south of Aberdeen where the Slessors had lived previously. It is famous for its jute factories, linen weaving, ship-building—and cakes! Here Mary went to work in a mill at an age when boys and girls of today are just leaving the Junior School to go into a Secondary School. Her hours were long and her earnings small, while the conditions in which she worked would not be allowed today for grown-ups. (This kind of thing was one of the causes of the Revolutions.)

For a year or two Mary worked at a loom for part of the day and went to school for the rest of it. But at an age much earlier than school life ends now she was working in the mill full time, and that meant from six o'clock in the morning until six o'clock in the evening. Twelve hours of every day were spent in dark, dirty sheds, amid an almost deafening noise. Her mother was greatly distressed at her daughter having to work so hard, but Mary does not seem to have minded very much. She was not the type of girl who was always grumbling. On the contrary she was cheerful and always ready with a smile and helping hand for others. She wasted no time, for as she worked at the loom she propped a book in front of her and

trained herself to read as she worked. She was not
the first to study at her work. Some 35 years
before a Scottish boy named David Livingstone
had done the very same thing. He had become a
doctor and by this time, about 1860, had become
a famous missionary and explorer. He had been
to scores of places in the Dark Continent, as Africa
was called, places where no white man had ever
been before. Among his discoveries were the
lovely Victoria Falls and some of the huge inland
lakes of that land.

Mary heard a good deal about Livingstone at
her church, the Wishart Church, named after a
great Scottish preacher named George Wishart.
He had preached near the site of the Church more
than 300 years before, in 1544, shortly before he
was burned to death for being a Christian. But
the part of Africa which interested Mary most
was called Calabar, where missionaries of the
Church of Scotland had been working since 1846.
Mary even began to wonder if the game of her
childhood—preaching to the dolls—might one
day become a reality. The thought caused her to
study harder than ever. There were no public
libraries then from which books could be bor-
rowed, but Mary obtained all she required from
friends or from the Sunday School library. In this
way she read all kinds of books, including Milton's
Paradise Lost and Carlyle's *Sartor Resartus,* in which
she became so absorbed that the time just flew
by as she read it. Her favourite book was the
Bible and, like many others who have not had

much schooling, she learned from its style how to write really well herself.

Through the influence of a Christian woman, a widow who lived near the Slessors, Mary came to understand what being a Christian really meant and was filled with a burning desire to win others for Christ. The Wishart Church was in a poor, rough part of Dundee, surrounded by narrow streets and passages (locally called "pends") which led to dreary tenement houses, where large families lived in overcrowded conditions.

Among these unfortunate folk Mary began her Christian witness. The Church had opened a Mission in one particularly bad area and she went to the Superintendent, offering herself as a Sunday School teacher. He thought the sensitive-looking girl would find the people too rough for her and tried to discourage her. But Mary was not easily put off. By nature shy and timid—she would often hide in a doorway at the sight of a dog—she was given by God a courage which made her ready to face anything that came her way, in Dundee first and then later on in Africa.

There was one young ruffian in particular who threatened to harm her if she did not give up her work; but she was quite undaunted. When he produced from his pocket a piece of string with a heavy lead weight on one end, she stood perfectly still. He began to whirl the weight round, bringing it closer to Mary's face each time until it almost grazed her forehead. Still she stood there unflinching and smiling, waiting for the blow which would have knocked her senseless to the ground. Suddenly the young tough became ashamed of his bullying; he flicked the weight away and followed Mary into the Mission with several of his companions.

On another occasion a boy with a whip appeared at the door of the Mission.

"Suppose we changed places," Mary asked him, "what would happen?"

"I would get this whip across my shoulders," he replied.

"I will bear it for you," answered Mary, "if you'll go in." He threw away his whip and followed her into the Mission. Many of these boys were converted and became Christian workers themselves.

Meanwhile sorrow had entered the Slessor family. The death of her father soon after their move to Dundee was not so great a loss as it would have been if he had been kinder to his children. The loss of four of her brothers and sisters was felt more keenly, especially the death of Robert, the one whose heart had been set on going to the mission field. The youngest boy, John, was sent to New Zealand for his health, only to die soon after his arrival.

Mrs. Slessor had greatly hoped that one of her children would become a missionary. She had expected that God would call Robert to the work. Now she was to learn that God does not often do what we expect Him to do. Robert He took to be with Himself, but Mary heard His call as she worked at her looms, thinking about the needs of the millions of coloured folk in Africa who had never heard of the Saviour whom she knew as her Friend and loved so dearly.

Gradually she came to feel more and more sure that God wanted her to go to Calabar, on the west coast of Africa, known then as "the White Man's Grave," because few white folk ever lived long enough in its treacherous climate. Her main worry was about her mother and her two remaining sisters. How would they manage without the small wage which she brought home each week? When she realised that she would be able to make them an allowance out of her salary she acted quickly, making the second great decision of her life (the first, of course, was when she accepted the Lord Jesus as her own Saviour). At about the time that Mary was making up her mind to offer herself for Calabar, news reached Scotland that David Livingstone had died. He had blazed a trail across the Continent of Africa and his death called urgently for others to pick up the torch he had laid down and to carry on the noble work of healing and preaching the Gospel which he had begun. Mary Slessor was to be one of them.

Her mother was overjoyed when she heard of Mary's decision and assured her that she would make a fine missionary. In 1875 she wrote to the Foreign Mission Board of the Church of Scotland and, after a long wait—they probably wanted to make sure she was not going to change her mind—was accepted as a teacher for the work in Calabar.

II

CALABAR

Boys and girls who collect stamps usually have a good knowledge of geography, but even they may wonder just where Calabar is. They certainly will not find such a country in their stamp album. That is because it is not really a country in itself, but only part of one.

In the south-east corner of the British colony of Nigeria—see if you can find it on a map—and near to that part of Africa where the coastline, after running from west to east for many hundreds of miles, suddenly turns southwards, is an estuary. That means the mouth of a river in which the tide comes in twice daily just as the sea does at the seaside. The river which flows into the estuary is the Cross River and, near the mouth, it has a tributary called the Calabar River, which gives its name to that particular corner of Nigeria.

From the beach of this estuary rise steep cliffs, with buildings on the sides and tops. This is the town of Calabar, and a little to the south, in a valley between the hills, lies Duke Town where most of the natives live. Thanks to the tide, quite large ships can reach the port of Calabar, and for many years there has been a regular service from there to Liverpool.

In the days when slave traders used to raid the coast of Africa to obtain negroes, whom they sold into slavery on the other side of the Atlantic, this area was the one which suffered worst. When slavery was done away with, there were left behind in Calabar some of the most degraded people on the face of the earth. Very few of them were free men. Most were slaves of the chiefs. It was among these people that the Church of Scotland missionaries had been working for thirty years when Mary Slessor sailed from Liverpool to join their ranks on August 5, 1876.

The ship on which she sailed was called the *S.S. Ethiopia* and among her fellow passengers was an architect named Mr. Thomson. He was anxious to do what he could to help the missionaries and Mary had many a talk with him during the voyage. He told her all about the land to which she was going, of its beauty, of its wonderful tropical flowers, of strange wild animals, and birds with brilliantly coloured feathers. He also told her that it was very unhealthy, but that he had planned to build a rest home for the missionaries 5,000 feet up in the Cameroon Mountains where they could regain their health, far from the swamps where lurk the malaria-carrying mosquitoes. It was a fine idea but I am sorry to say that Mr. Thomson himself was taken ill and died before he could carry out his plan.

The voyage took about five weeks. Then, on September 11, the vessel steamed into the lovely estuary and Mary saw for the first time the palms, mangoes and other tropical trees of the land which was to be her home, the land with

which her name is forever linked. On the sand-
banks she could see cranes and pelicans and
crocodiles. It was a thrilling moment for her as
she stepped ashore on African soil, but a sad one,
for, as she looked around her, she saw the casks
of drink sent out from Europe for the natives.
She could not help but think of the trouble which
drink had caused in her own home. "Scores of
casks," she remarked, "but only one missionary."

So this was Calabar, the land of which she had
dreamed for so long. And these natives who
gathered around the port, gazing at the new
arrivals from the land of the white man were the
Efiks, a tribe which had come to the area from
the neighbourhood of the Niger River about 150
years before. Their coming followed a civil war
in which much blood had been shed. It was said
that there was not a single Efik man who was not
descended from slaves.

The first missionary from Scotland was a man
named Hope Waddell. Among his assistants was
William Anderson who, with his wife, now
welcomed Mary. Soon they were telling her about
the people whom she was to teach. They were
cruel and wicked and lived in fear of a secret
society called Ekpo, membership of which could
only be obtained by payment of money and a
sacrifice in which blood was shed. Sometimes the
missionaries had witnessed terrible scenes of
violence, the worst of which took place at the
funeral of a king called Egamba.

Mary learned that the Efiks were very useful to

traders from Europe. They made contact with the tribes who lived further inland and obtained from them the palm oil which the traders wanted, but they would not allow these natives to come through their villages to take the goods direct to the traders. In this way they made sure that they kept a handsome profit for themselves. Captains of trading ships for their part were in the habit of making a big fuss of the more important natives, those whom they could trust to do what they wanted. They used to call them "kings" and pay them well for all the palm oil which passed through their hands.

As Mary listened to all this, she wondered how she was going to get on among such strange people. She was specially interested when the Andersons spoke of the tribes further up the river. No one had yet ventured among them with the Gospel and Mary felt a great longing to have that honour herself. It was to win such savages for Christ that she had left her native land and her dear ones.

But first of all she had to learn patience—and the language. Impetuous and lively by nature she found life with the Andersons a bit irksome. They, in their turn, must have been rather surprised at the new helper who had been sent out to them. She ran races with the native boys and girls, climbed trees like a boy, and went for long walks in the bush, finding endless pleasure in the wonderful tropical plants and birds. Sometimes she would arrive back late from these expeditions and would be sent to bed without any supper by Mrs. Anderson, just as though she were a naughty child. When this happened, Mr. Anderson would usually talk his wife into letting him take her some bananas and biscuits so that she would not be kept awake by hunger.

Before long she claimed that she had climbed "every tree that was worth climbing" for miles around the Mission, yet she never forgot the first purpose of her life which was to win the savage folk around her for Christ. As she worked hard at the language and kept herself fit and strong with her boisterous activities, she was always thinking of the tribes in the unexplored bush, enslaved by cruel and wicked customs, who had never yet heard the Name of Jesus. She curbed her patience, remembering that she had once heard someone say, "Jesus was never in a hurry."

She was deeply shocked to learn what happened when a native chief died; it was the custom to cut off the heads of his wives and his slaves and to bury them with him. She learned that slaves were branded with a hot iron to show to whom they belonged, that many of them had their ears cut off, and that girls were fattened up like animals to be sold as slave wives. She was especially upset when she heard what happened when twins were born. It was believed among the natives that the father of one of the twins was an evil spirit. As they did not know which twin it was, both had to be killed and the mother banished. The backs of the poor, innocent babies were broken, their bodies crushed to pieces, placed in jars, and taken from the hut where they were born, not through the door, but through a hole specially cut in the rear. Meanwhile, their mother would be thrown into the bush and left to die of starvation or be killed by wild beasts. There are times when we do well to be really angry and the thought of these cruelties roused Mary to say, "I shall fight this. It must be stopped . . . I will never give up."

Before long Mary's childhood longing became a reality and she had around her real coloured boys and girls listening to the wonderful stories of the Bible. "Ma" Slessor they called her, "Ma" being a term of respect in the Efik language.

She was soon able to visit the people in their homes. One Sunday she came upon an old man, sitting outside his hut. She knew him, for he usually attended the Sunday services at the Mission. "Why are you not on the way to God's House?" she asked him. He replied that his heart was sad for his only child had died and "even now is buried in the house." Opening her Bible, Mary read to him the story of Jesus bringing Lazarus back to life. Especially she stressed the words, "I am the resurrection and the life. If a man believeth in Me, though he were dead, yet shall he live" (John 11:25). At last the old man began to find comfort. "Well," he said, "if God has taken him, it is not so bad."

Among the friends she made in the early days was a headman who was known as King Eyo

Honesty VII. He had become a Christian and Mary was deeply impressed by his earnestness and sincerity. She knew that her mother had heard of him and she now suggested that King Eyo should write to Mrs. Slessor. The result was that for several years these two exchanged letters with each other. It must be one of the most unusual and interesting examples of a pen friendship that there ever was.

After three years of such work, the unhealthy climate began to tell on the young missionary. She became ill and in her sickness longed for the cold damp of Dundee with its skies so often overcast with clouds. Missionaries call their well-earned holidays in the homeland furlough, and Mary was now due for her first furlough. In June, 1879, she went aboard the steamer which was to take her home. Many of her coloured friends came to the quay to wave goodbye as she sailed away. She was not, of course, going home for good, only for a rest and to see her friends and loved ones. When she had regained her health and strength, she would be coming back ready to make far greater conquests for Christ in Calabar than ever she had dreamed of in her childhood.

III

TOWARDS THE FORESTS

SHE was in Scotland for just over a year, during which she visited a number of churches to tell

Christians of the great needs of Africa. Because of her shyness she found it difficult to speak in public, but once she had started, the burden of the terrible evils of heathenism seemed to inspire her. Often she roused her hearers to feel that they must do something to send the light to the dark land of Calabar. In Falkirk she spoke to a girls' Bible class, leaving such a deep impression that six of the girls went out to Calabar when they grew up.

She found her mother in poor health, but before she went back to Africa she found a new home for her and her two sisters in a village outside Dundee, where they would be away from the smoke and dirt of the city.

In the autumn of 1880 she sailed again for her adopted land, together with two of the pioneer missionaries, also returning from furlough, Rev. and Mrs. Hugh Goldie. On arrival in Calabar, she was overjoyed to be given more responsibility, the charge of the Mission at Old Town. It was only two miles from Duke Town where she had been before, but it was two miles nearer the forests, where lived the tribes who had never heard the Gospel.

Her new home was just a hut made from bamboo sticks and mud, with mats for a roof. Its mud walls were simply whitewashed. She ate the same food as the natives—yams, which look like enormous potatoes and can be kept for a long time before they go bad, and plantains, a fruit similar to bananas. In this way she was able to live very cheaply and send most of her salary home for her mother and sisters.

Mary was never very worried about what we call convention; that means doing what is supposed to be the correct thing. People were sometimes shocked by the unexpected things she did, but she knew that God did not mind when she took off her shoes and stockings and accustomed herself to walking everywhere barefoot, nor when she had her auburn hair cut short and parted like a boy's.

She now had opportunity to do something about the twins. Before she had been at Old Town long, she rescued a pair and brought them to live with her at the mission house. The natives watched carefully to see what would happen, quite sure that the white woman must be a friend of the Devil and that some dreadful disaster would take place. When nothing happened, some of them began to think that perhaps their beliefs had been foolish, but it was going to be a long time before they would grow out of them. From this time on for the rest of her life, Mary always had around her a little family of rescued children.

One day a Scottish trader arrived at the Mission, bringing with him a baby girl he had found in the forest. She was one of twins, the other having died. "This one would soon have died too," he said, "but I know how you feel about these little ones, so I brought her to you." Mary called her Janie after one of her sisters, and from that day on looked after her as though she had been her own child.

When slaves died, leaving young children, no one wanted the bother of looking after them and they were usually killed like the twins. Mary started to rescue these as well. Before long she had her hands full with rescued children and mothers of twins and had to appeal for someone else to help her.

There were other things which also roused her anger. The tribe which lived near the coast had been allowed to make their homes there by another tribe which lived a little further inland. Then the new arrivals, instead of being grateful, would not allow the inland tribe to bring their palm oil and other products to market. This was because they were greedy for the money which they could get for handling the goods themselves. Often there was fighting and bloodshed. What Mary did was to help the inland tribe by showing them a secret path by which they could bring their palm oil to the European traders.

It is said that an ounce of practice is worth a pound of preaching. This means that preaching the Gospel can do little good if those who preach do not live real Christian lives, following the example of their Master who "went about doing good." This Mary certainly did, taking medicine with her as she went out among the people, and finding that the wall of opposition was far more easily broken down by the giving of medical treatment than by hours of preaching on Sundays.

Gradually she began to see results. One joyful and long to be remembered night she was sitting on her verandah with her children around, when the noise of beating drums and singing men was heard. A proclamation was being made and as she listened Mary heard that from that day on all twins and their mothers were to be allowed to live; in fact, anyone who harmed them was to be hanged. You will not be surprised to hear that Mary wept tears of joy as she heard the news. A few days later, papers giving effect to the new law were publicly signed, while some of the twins' mothers were sitting on the platform. The revolution had certainly begun.

So great was the noise while the signing was going on that Mary asked a local chief to make the people be quiet. "Ma," he replied, "how can I stop them women mouths? How can I do it? They be women." It was no wonder the women were so glad, for none of them knew which of them would be the next to be so unfortunate as to became a mother of twins. Mary wrote a most interesting letter home describing the great occasion. In her letter she told her friends what the people were wearing. Some wore pants but no shirts; others wore uniforms with gold and silver lace; while others were wearing tablecloths and beads! The men of the secret society called Ekpo wore three-cornered hats with long plumes. Some wore masks and horns of animals and skirts with yards of material trailing behind. It certainly must have been a strange and unforgettable sight.

But the missionaries' work was only just beginning. The people had given up one of their dreadful customs. They had not become Christians. Only Christ can help men to throw off the shackles of sin. The enthusiasm and excitement wore off. Reports came in to the Mission that in outlying villages twins were still being cruelly killed, so hard is it for men and women to change the habits of generations.

News of Mary's work spread to tribes further away up the river. One of these tribes was ruled over by a chief called King Okon. He sent messengers, asking the white lady to visit his people. When her old friend, King Eyo Honesty VII heard of this, he said she must use his royal canoe. Preparations were accordingly made for the journey. When the long, narrow, brightly-painted canoe was ready, crowds of Mary's new friends gathered on the beach to say goodbye to her and to wish her well. She seated herself in the middle of the canoe, beneath an awning which protected her from the hot sun. Flags flew at the prow. Thirty-three men, wearing only loin cloths, were needed to paddle the boat. It was late afternoon before they started and they had not gone far before darkness fell. On they rowed all night, singing a song, the verses of which they made up as they went along. After each verse came a chorus which went something like this:

Ma, our beautiful, beloved mother, is
     on board.
Ho! Ho! Ho!

The singing lulled Mary to sleep. When she awoke day was dawning and they were getting near King Okon's village. Their arrival was greeted with a great shout of welcome. Mary went ashore and was taken to the hut set aside for

her. It was a very simple guest-house, with no
door, only a piece of cotton cloth hanging over the
entrance to give her a little privacy. Rats, lizards
and insects crawled or ran around the floor, while
the fat, perspiring wives of the chief sat as near
to her as possible, this being regarded as polite
behaviour!

Never before had any of these people seen a
white woman. Out of curiosity they came along
to watch everything she did. They touched her
to see what she felt like. They pinched her. They
gazed at her in apparent amazement when she
ate her food.

All this must have been very unpleasant for the
shy, Scottish girl, but Mary put up with the
inconvenience for the sake of her Lord, for whom
she longed to win these people. She handed out
medicine to the sick. She taught the women how
to sew. She tried to make them cleaner in their
habits. Above all, every day, she told them about
the Lord Jesus and His great love for them. On
Sundays she spread a white cloth over a table, on
which she placed a Bible, a hymn book and some
flowers. Crowds would then gather around to
hear what she had to say. When the service
finished they made their way home along jungle
paths where Mary, always ready for adventure,
wanted to follow them. But King Okon would not
allow that. It was "elephant country" he told her.
So much damage had the elephants caused in
their stampedes that the people had been forced
to give up their gardens and to live mainly on fish.

One morning, while Mary was praying, she heard a commotion outside the hut. A huge snake had appeared in the compound. She could remember the time when she had been frightened by a mouse. Now God was giving her courage, so that she did not fear either snakes strong enough to squeeze people to death or elephants which could pull up trees by the roots.

While she was in King Okon's village, two sixteen-year-old wives of the chief broke a strict rule. They went into a hut where a young boy was asleep and for this they were sentenced to be beaten. They were to receive a hundred lashes, after which salt would be rubbed into their bleeding backs to make the wounds more painful. Mary determined to do something for the girls. She pleaded with the chief, telling him they were young and simply loved a bit of fun. The chief listened to her politely. Then he told her that Christianity was no good if it stopped the punishment of those who broke laws. Mary knew there was some truth in this and she spoke words of reproof to the two girls, after which she rounded on the chief and the older men, telling them that they were to blame for having bad laws and cruel customs, for allowing girls of sixteen to marry, and for their practice of polygamy (the having of more than one wife). Eventually the sentence was reduced from a hundred lashes to ten. When the flogging was over, Mary took the girls into her hut, treating their wounds and telling them of the One who was "wounded for our transgressions

and bruised for our iniquities." The girls drank
in the message, as did the crowd which gathered
outside.

At last the time came for Mary to return to
Old Town. On the night of her journey back down
the river there was a terrible storm. Mary was
soaked to the skin and in the morning was very ill.
For several weeks she was unable to do any work
at all. Then, just as she was beginning to feel a
little better, the town was hit by a tornado, a
storm accompanied by a violent wind. The roof
of her hut was blown right off and she was once
again soaked while trying to keep her children
dry. This made her very ill once more and it was
decided that she must go back to Scotland for a
complete rest.

She had by this time grown particularly fond
of Janie, the little girl who had been brought to
her by the trader, and she decided to take the child
with her. She feared, too, that if she left Janie
behind, the wicked people who still wanted to
murder all twins would kidnap her and kill her.
In April, 1883, Mary Slessor, with her little
dark-skinned baby, set sail for Liverpool.

IV

A PIONEER AMONG SAVAGES

HER visit and the sight of the child aroused
tremendous interest wherever she went. So many
people wanted her to visit their churches to tell

of what God was doing in Calabar that she had
to remain in Britain longer than she had at first
expected. Her furlough also was saddened by the
death of one of her sisters and the ill health of
the other sister and of Mrs. Slessor. Mary thought
carefully about what she ought to do and eventually made arrangements for them to go and live
with some friends in Devon where the climate is
more pleasant than in Dundee.

Soon after her return to Africa, however, first
her mother and then her sister were taken to be
with the Lord Jesus, and Mary was then left
alone in the world, with only Janie to remind her
of the last few months with her loved ones. Her
mother had from the first encouraged her in her
desire to be a missionary and then had prayed for
her constantly; and Mary always felt that the
wonderful things which God did through her in
Calabar would never have been done but those
at home who upheld her in prayer.

These losses only made her more willing to give
her all in Christ's service. "Heaven is now nearer
to me than Britain," she said, "and there is no
one to be anxious about me if I go up country."

And up country she went. Soon after her return
to Africa, it was decided to open up work further
inland and Mary was chosen to be the pioneer.
She was to go to the bush country of Okoyong,
an area lying between the rivers Cross and
Calabar.

The tribe to which she was going had customs
even more revolting and horrible than any she

had met with up till then. In addition to the
practice of twin-murder, they used poison beans
and boiling oil to kill and torture their victims.
They used to lie in wait along the bush paths to
kill anyone who came their way. They raided
other tribes and stole their slaves. The rule of the
British Government had not then reached that far
and Mary found herself facing one of the toughest
jobs that any woman had ever faced. The thoughts
of the tasks ahead drove her to pray more earnestly than ever before; and from the Lord in whom
she put her trust she received strength and courage
to go forward. She had peace in her heart, knowing that if these people were to kill her, she would
go to be with her Lord. She had no relatives to
mourn for her and there was always the thought
that maybe God would use her to bring an end
to the barbarities which had been carried on for
centuries. She wrote letters to friends at home
asking them to pray for her in this new venture.
At the same time she did not want them to spend
long hours uttering flowery prayers. "Pray in a
business-like manner," she said.

When the time came for her to go up country
to make arrangements for the opening of the new
outpost, King Eyo once again lent his royal
canoe. What is more, he provided a carpet,
cushions and curtains, so that she would be more
comfortable and have some privacy on the long
journey. Her food for the trip consisted of home-
made bread and tinned meat. She had with her a
small paraffin stove on which she made tea.

As the boat skimmed through the water, she was delighted and thrilled with the beauty of her surroundings. The banks of the river were lined with stately trees, palms, bananas and many other tropical plants.

The village to which she was going was called Ekenge. It was not on the river and Mary had to walk four miles through the bush to reach it. The people came out of their huts to welcome her, crowding around and calling her "Ma." They seemed pleased that she had come to their village and the chief, whose name was Edem, put a hut at her disposal for the night. Soon Mary was proclaiming the Gospel to these folk who had never before heard such a strange story. She tried to impress upon them that the Christian way of life would bring great happiness to their village.

Most of the night she lay awake, not so much because she was on a strange bed as because she was on an uncomfortable one. Some sticks, covered with dirty corn, laid down in a hut infested with rats and insects, do not make an ideal bed on which to sleep. When we learn that alongside her lay three fat women and a three-week old baby and that just outside the hut were numerous animals—goats, sheep, cows and dogs— it is hardly surprising that she slept little. We can imagine her lying there, wondering what the future held for this most backward part of Africa and praying that God would use her to change the lives and customs of these strange people.

About two miles away was another village

called Ifako. Mary visited there also and impressed the headman by her charm and by her desire to help his people. He and Edem promised that they would allow her to start work in their villages and each undertook to provide land for a school and a church. They also agreed that the mission buildings and the missionary's home were to be places of refuge for natives accused of witchcraft and other crimes.

She seems from the first to have taken a liking to the people among whom she was going to live in spite of their many terrible customs. They were of stronger build and finer looking than the people of the coastal area and Mary was quick to realise that underneath their dark skins lay uncommon strength of character. "They are proud, brave and independent," she wrote, "and will make good soldiers of Christ when they have learned to love Him."

During the return journey, the canoe was delayed by a sudden storm which caused the tide to turn unexpectedly against them. The waves breaking against the hollow tree trunk gave the missionary a soaking. Being wet, combined with the rocking motion, made it difficult for her to sleep, so she watched the river for crocodiles. She saw a large snake swim past, also a dead body floating with the stream. The natives who loved their white mistress continually whispered to one another such things as "Don't shake the canoe or you will wake Ma" and "Don't talk so loud so Ma can sleep." At last the boat floated more evenly and the weary missionary fell into a deep sleep.

The next few weeks were filled with preparations for the extension of the work. King Eyo not only promised her his canoe again, but provided a party of bearers to carry the luggage from the landing beach to the village. When the time came for her to leave, a great crowd of her coloured friends gathered to bid her God-speed. One of them reminded her that she was facing death by going to live among so savage a tribe, but this woman, once so timid that on Guy Fawkes night she would stay indoors rather than mingle with excited crowds, now knew no fear, for her God had clearly promised, "Fear thou not for I am with thee." The Christian natives promised to pray for her, the first white person to be allowed to go among the peoples of Okoyong. With her went five of the children whom she had rescued from death and another missionary, a Mr. Bishop, who was to stay with her for a few days until her home was established.

As they sailed away, her thoughts were full of the great things which she believed Christ was about to do. She was only one woman, going among thousands of heathens, but, like the apostle Paul, she knew that through Christ she could do all things.

Once again it was the wet season and when it rains in Calabar it is nothing like the showery rain which we have in Britain almost all the year round. There the rain teems down in torrents,

soaking everyone and everything. It was a full
day's journey up the river, but Mary had sent a
message to Chief Edem and hoped that there
would be bearers to meet her to help carry the
luggage through the four miles of forest.

When the boat came to the landing place,
however, there was no one to be seen. Darkness
was falling and it was pouring with rain. Leaving
Mr. Bishop to arrange the unloading, Mary set
off on the long walk through the bush. It was a
strange procession which wound its way along.
She carried the youngest child, a baby, on her
back, while the other four tramped along behind.
The oldest child, a boy of eleven, carried on his
head a box containing tea, sugar and bread. One
of the others carried a kettle and cooking pots. All
the children were wet through and thoroughly
miserable. But worse was to follow. When they
reached Ekenge, the village seemed to be deserted.
It turned out that everyone had gone to Ifako to
attend the funeral of the chief's mother. This
meant that they would all spend several days
feasting, drinking, dancing and fighting.

Mary lost no time in lighting a fire beside which
the children could get warm and dry their clothes.
Then she made tea and waited for the bearers
to arrive with the luggage. It was a long wait and
then a messenger arrived with the news that the
men supplied by King Eyo were much too frightened to make their way through the bush at night.
In fact they had gone on strike, announcing that
they would stay where they were until morning.

Needing food and dry clothes urgently, Mary sent the messenger back to order the natives to come on at once. Then, tired as she was, she decided that she had better go herself. Barefooted, she set out on the long walk back to the landing beach. From time to time she was startled by weird noises coming from among the trees, but she believed that God was protecting her and went on until she reached the river. She next waded out to the canoe, wakened the sleeping natives and persuaded them to carry out her wishes. That they did so shows us what a wonderful personality Mary Slessor possessed, getting these men to do for her what they would have done for no one else.

The circumstances were not very promising for the beginning of the work in Ekenge. Mr. Bishop and the natives sent by King Eyo did not stay long. They went back to Creek Town and Mary was left alone with the savage tribe. Daily she went into the forest and cut down trees to build herself a hut and to make some simple furniture. Her chief helper was an eleven-year-old boy, the son of a headman, but she did most of the hard work herself. It is the more remarkable when we remember that Mary lived at a time when women were regarded as weak creatures, quite unfit to do the same kind of work as men.

When the natives came back from the funeral ceremonies, Mary's help was needed for one of the wives of the chief. She had been bitten by her husband and a wound had been caused which was not healing. Mary took it in hand and as the wound healed the woman and the chief began to show signs of friendliness. Others came to her with various ailments. Mary remembered that her Master had gone about healing the sick and thus reaching many who would not otherwise have heard His message. She was glad that in this respect at any rate she was able to follow in His steps. The work of healing has always been one of the first tasks of Christian missionaries and all over the world has been the means of making friends and opening doors for the preaching of the Gospel.

Among visitors who came to see the strange white woman were some warriors, notorious all through that part of Nigeria for their fierce and warlike behaviour. Leaving their weapons outside Mary's hut, they came to see her like a deputation of civilised gentlemen.

Enormous interest was shown in Mary's simple possessions. No one had ever before seen a clock, an organ or a sewing machine. Her clothes, bedding and curtains were greatly admired by the women, while the men would have given almost anything for the piece of glass which she used as a window, her door hinges, bedroom furniture and meat safe. All these curiosities attracted astonished sightseers and Mary seized every such opportunity to tell her visitors about the Lord Jesus, who had sent her to their land.

But Mary was to have many sad experiences among these people. The boy who had become so friendly and had helped her to build her hut was accused of giving up the customs of his tribe. One day he was cruelly tortured in an attempt to stop him from seeing so much of the missionary. Boiling oil was poured over his hands and arms, much to the grief of Mary who arrived just too late to prevent it. Boiling oil was often used in this way at trials, the chiefs excusing themselves by pretending that if the accused party was not guilty it would not hurt him! Mary made up her mind that with God's help she would put an end to this fearful practice.

And there were worse evils than this for her to fight. She soon discovered the dreadful hold which belief in witchcraft, had on the people. When a chief died it was the custom to kill his wives and slaves, so that he would not be alone in the place to which he had gone. If it was decided that his death had been caused by witchcraft, many more people would be killed, often after fearful torture.

Chief Edem had a sister with whom Mary was very friendly. Her name was Ma Eme. One day she told Mary the story of her life. She had been married to a great chief. After his death, all his wives had been accused of using witchcraft to bring it about. Each had had to bring a chicken to the trial. The head of the chicken was then cut off and the headless fowl was placed on the head of the accused woman. The direction in which the chicken fluttered to the ground decided the guilt or innocence of the accused. Ma Eme had fainted with shock when the witch doctor pronounced her not guilty as her fowl fluttered to the ground.

Soon after Mary had settled at Ekenge, a request came to her to visit a village about eight miles away to attend the chief who was very sick. Mary thought the matter over carefully and decided that this was a wonderful opportunity to carry the Gospel where the Name of Christ had never before been heard. Chief Edem and Ma Eme did not want her to go, but they, of course, did not know her all-powerful God who could look after her anywhere. They warned her of the dangers of the journey, which would mean her crossing some flooded rivers. They thus hoped to prevent her from going. Their real fear was that the chief might die. Then there would be riots. People would be murdered. It was possible that the missionary might be held to blame. Mary's point of view was that the chief might die if she did not go. Then his wives, slaves and possibly others would be killed. If her treatment made him better, these lives would be saved. On the other hand she realised that his death, if she went, might cause a war between the two tribes. She did not want to do anything which might cause bloodshed. She, therefore, prayed that God would make clear what He wished her to do. As she prayed she became really sure that God wanted her to go. It meant an argument with Chief Edem, but he gave in in the end and provided Mary with a guide and a guard.

To make the journey worse it was pouring with rain. The tropical heat added to the discomfort of wet clothes. At last Mary could bear the unpleasantness of her damp clothes no longer and she took most of them off. There was a small village through which she had to pass, where the people stood at the entrances to their huts and watched in silence this strange sight of a half clad white woman trudging through the bush. Mary was afraid they might despise her and that this would bring dishonour to her Lord, but they, knowing the purpose of her journey, admired her extraordinary courage.

On arrival at the village, she was given some dirty rags to wear in place of her soaked garments. It was not pleasant for her to put these things on, but Mary did so for the sake of Him in whose service she delighted. She found the village in a state of tremendous tension. All were expecting the chief to die. Some expected to be put to death in the riots that would follow. Others were looking forward to taking part in the murders. She went in to see the chief and found him very seriously ill indeed. Day after day she nursed him, while she prayed more earnestly than ever as she realised how much depended on the outcome of the illness. Her careful attention and prayers led to the chief's recovery and a desire on the part of his people to learn what they called simply "book." They promised her that they would make peace with other tribes and she promised to send them a teacher as soon as possible.

V

FIGHTING HEATHEN CUSTOMS

WHEN she arrived back in Ekenge, she found Chief Edem very ill. He had a painful abscess on his back. Fastened to a stick in the middle of the room was a live fowl; scattered around were eggs and feathers; hanging round the sick man's neck and arms were charms placed there by the witch doctor. When Mary reproved him for his superstition and belief in witchcraft, Edem produced a curious collection of things which were supposed to have been removed from the abscess. These things, he said, proved that an enemy had caused the abscess. This meant that more cruelties would be carried out. In all probability, innocent men and women would be chained at posts and made to take poison or would have boiling oil poured over them.

Mary did her utmost to prevent these things; but the chief, with his leading counsellors, wives and prisoners, was taken to a farm where the missionary was not allowed to visit him. In this crisis there was only one thing she could do. She prayed that God would step in to prevent these dreadful crimes. After some days Edem began to recover. The murder of the prisoners was postponed, but his recovery was celebrated with a wild orgy of feasting and dancing.

One day a chief from a neighbouring tribe came on a visit to Ekenge. The event was an excuse for celebration in the usual way—the people drinking far more than was good for them, with the result that they became quarrelsome and called upon Mary to settle their arguments. Her chief fear was that the men would become so drunk that they would be out of control. She was anxious for the visit to end. When the day of departure did arrive, the whole village was in a state of tremendous excitement. Guns were being fired and drawn swords were being waved about rather alarmingly.

Even so, the day might have passed uneventfully had not the visitors suddenly caught sight of a plantain shoot with some withered palm leaves, nuts and a cocoanut shell lying near their path. This was regarded as the work of a sorcerer and had been done with the object of casting an evil spell on them. At once the men ran off towards the nearest village, shouting out that the people who lived there had tried to bewitch them. So well did Mary know the paths through the bush that when she found she could not overtake them, she went by a short cut which enabled her to get ahead and stand in their path. What could one woman do against a party of strong men, maddened by stupid beliefs and half drunk? The only answer that Mary knew lay in prayer and she prayed hard that the intended crime might be prevented. Amazed at the courage of the little white woman, the savage, half drunk negroes argued with her, but at last were persuaded not to go on. They returned with Mary to the place where what they called the "sorcery medicine" had been put. They were still afraid, however, to pass it until she picked it up and threw it into the bush. The men were horrified at her action, though they admired her bravery.

When the men arrived at their own village, they drank still more and then started fighting among themselves. Once again Mary stepped in. With the help of those who were sober she tied some of the worst ones to trees until the effects of the drink wore off! On the way home she picked up the offending plantain shoot for planting in her own garden to show the people how harmless was their much feared "magic."

But Mary had not heard the last of the incident. Next morning a runner arrived demanding the offending shoot. Fearing that to refuse his request might lead to bloodshed, Mary sent it. The savage chief then sent for the people of the village which he blamed for trying to bewitch him. He made them swear solemnly that they had not tried to do him harm and captured one of their young men as a hostage. Mary was now called in by the villagers to get their young man back. She pleaded with the chief but in vain. He merely laughed in her face. Describing the incident she wrote afterwards, "Had God not been with me I would have been killed." The only thing she could now do was to pray and where pleading with the negro chief had failed pleading with her God prevailed. Without explanation the young man was set free and sent back to his people.

At this time Mary was living in very crowded quarters. She had her five rescued children, three boys and two girls, sharing her little hut. At night everything that could be moved was carried outside to make room for them all to sleep. Nor had she much privacy or quiet, for close to her hut were the quarters of the chief's head wife, his five lesser wives, also numerous other wives less important still, slaves and children.

In addition to all this crowd, her hut was hemmed around with animals—goats, cows, hens, dogs and cats, to say nothing of the rats—so that she must have felt as though she were in the middle of a farmyard all the time. She made the best of these circumstances with extraordinary cheerfulness, saying it was too far to go to Calabar to lie down!

Living so close to the people, though trying at times, certainly gave her a wonderful opportunity to study their customs. "Had I not my Saviour close beside me," she wrote, "I would have lost my reason." Sometimes she would slip away and hide herself behind a bush where she could feel alone with the Lord.

Her greatest friend at this time was the chief's sister, Ma Eme. She often cooked meals for her and kept her in touch with what was going on. Mary thought a great deal of her, though Ma Eme never actually renounced heathenism to accept Christ.

It was not at Ekenge, however, but at Ifako that the first Christian church in the district was built and Mary saw to it that no slaves were used in the work. Slavery was an evil which, as a Christian, she must fight against. It would seriously hinder the struggle against evil if slaves were allowed to work on the building of a church. Fortunately, there was no lack of voluntary help. Even the chiefs lent a hand, while their wives carried from the river the mats which had been sent up from the coast to form the roof. They also plastered the walls and cleaned the building.

It was a red letter day for the missionary when the church was opened. Nearly everyone came to the service and listened attentively to what was said. The chiefs made solemn promises that the building would always be regarded as sacred; that no warlike weapons would be carried into it; that it would be recognised as a place of refuge for accused people; and that they would send their wives and children to school there.

It gave Mary especial pleasure that the people had all washed for the great occasion; that they had had their dirty, matted hair cut off; and they seemed to realise that they were dedicating a house of God. She next taught them that Sunday was a special day when they should put on clean clothes, rest from their work and worship God.

When Mary started her school, nearly all the people attended for the first few days. They crowded together on the floor and watched in amazement as she held up cards on which were letters of the alphabet. They thought these were strange pictures and wondered what it was all leading to. Mary, of course, was giving them their first lesson in reading.

The grown-ups could not continue coming to school every day for long. They had work to do in the fields growing their food. But there were about thirty boys and girls who came regularly and within a surprisingly short time she was able to report that all the people knew the alphabet, while some could spell words of two syllables.

When school finished at Ifako, Mary would hurry through the bush to Ekenge to teach the people there. School being held there in the evening, all who wanted to could come and many availed themselves of the opportunity.

Adjoining the church at Ifako were two rooms in which Mary could sleep and eat if she wanted to stay there overnight; but she still continued to live in Ekenge, where Chief Edem had promised her a house. Whenever she reminded him of this promise, an excuse was always found to postpone the building. In the end Mary took matters into her own hands. With the help of the children she cleared a space in the bush. The sight of the white woman and her rescued children thus working stirred the natives to action and before long there was built a two-roomed bungalow with a veran-dah and store shed. The main building materials used were bamboo sticks and mud, while the furniture was made from mud dried hard in the hot sun. We who are used to much greater luxury may feel sorry for the missionary in her discomfort, but Mary professed to be very cosy in her new home. Her Master had had nowhere to lay His head and for His sake a few discomforts mattered little to her.

In a letter home which was published in the *Missionary Record* she described the house as "a beautiful building but lacking doors and windows as there is no carpenter to do this work." At the time that this item of news from Calabar was published there was in Edinburgh a Mr. Charles Ovens. He was a carpenter by trade and he was on the point of leaving Scotland to go to America when he heard that the Church was appealing for a carpenter to go to Calabar. Like Mary herself, he had longed from childhood to become a missionary and he at once volunteered for the work. About three months later he reached Ekenge, arriving while Mary, barefoot and surrounded by her children, was having dinner. We can imagine how grateful she was to God for sending this helper and it was not long before Charles Ovens was hard at work on the new buildings and witnessing the growing influence which Mary was exerting over the natives.

Soon after his arrival, the son of Chief Edem died as the result of an accident. A youth of about twenty, he had been handling a large log of wood when it slipped and knocked him unconscious. He was brought to Mary, but in spite of all her care and attention he died of the injury. She knew that the natives believed that all accidents were caused by witchcraft and she was at once prepared for serious trouble. As she feared, there was at once an outbreak of violence. Many people were arrested and charged with using magic to bring about the young man's death.

Next the dead man was placed on a chair in a sitting position, a feathered headdress on his head, rings on his fingers and a whip in his hand. More than a score of women sat around singing, apparently to cheer him on his way into the next world. Twelve prisoners from a village near where the accident had occurred were chained to posts in the same hut as the corpse, three of them being mothers with babies in their arms. On constant guard were about fifty warriors, armed with swords and guns, and yelling all the time like a pack of demons.

Day and night Mary and Mr. Ovens took it in turns to remain on the scene. Never for one moment did they leave the hut, knowing that directly their backs were turned the massacre might begin. Once an attempt was made to kill one of the women by what was known as the poison ordeal. Some brown beans called esere beans were ground to powder and mixed with water. The prisoner then had to drink the mixture. As the beans were a deadly poison the drink naturally killed the victim, but the natives would say that if innocent the prisoner would not be harmed. The wretched woman had raised the cup of poison to her lips and was about to drink when Mary decided the time had come to act. She rushed up to the woman, caught hold of her hand, and, before the crowd of maddened natives realised what was happening, raced off with her to her own house, which you will remember the chief had promised to regard as a place of refuge.

One by one Mary tactfully obtained the release of the unhappy prisoners until only three remained, two of whom were related to the dead lad's mother and the other to the chief of the village which was accused of causing the magic. Edem flatly refused to let them go and was very angry with Mary for preventing him from carrying out the murders. It is even possible that he might have turned against her, had not two missionaries arrived from Duke Town, in answer to an urgent summons from Mary. The presence of two more white men, making four white people in their village at once deeply impressed the heathen chief. It proved the importance of his dead son. Two more prisoners were released, leaving only one, a woman. They were determined that she should die, but on the night arranged for the murder someone, possible Ma Eme, cut her chains and the poor woman was able to crawl to Mary's house and safety. In the end the body was safely buried without anyone being murdered. His only companion at the funeral was a cow! It was a marvellous triumph for the Gospel. Never before in that part of Africa had a person of importance been buried without scenes of bloodshed and torture.

The missionaries from Duke Town had brought with them a magic lantern and gave a show which excited the wonder of the whole population, making them forget that their custom had been frustrated.

The matter did not quite end there. Some weeks went by and then an uncle of the dead lad was accused of having caused the murder. The accused man demanded that he and other chiefs, including Edem himself, should undergo the ordeal of the poison beans. Mary was told of this—it was Ma Eme who kept her informed of all that was going on—and she acted quickly. She stole the bag of beans and kept them until everyone concerned had calmed down.

The chief of the accused village—his name was Akpo—was so grateful to Mary for all that she had done that he knelt before her and promised never to act against her wishes. Even Edem came round in the end and thanked her for preventing bloodshed at his son's funeral. "Your ways are better than ours," he said. "We are all weary of the old customs."

Another triumph followed soon afterwards of quite a different kind. As you have already heard, these people of Okoyong had never been on friendly terms with the natives living nearer the coast and had never traded with them. Now Mary set about breaking down this barrier. She showed them many little things such as mirrors and articles of clothing and explained that if they would undertake to be friendly with the coastal tribes, it would be possible for them to get some of these things themselves. Eventually she persuaded them to allow the Christian chief of Creek Town,

King Eyo, to mediate between them and their
old enemies. When they set off for the palaver
armed and ready for a fight, Mary told them they
must leave their weapons behind. They were
disgusted at this. "You want to make women of
us," they protested. "Would a man go among
strangers without arms?" When Mary insisted
that they were not to carry weapons, some of the
men went back to their homes, while the others
argued with her for hours. At last they gave in
and handed over their guns and swords. The
journey down the river began, but as they were
moving off Mary caught sight of the gleam of
swords hidden under the goods in the canoe. She
did not waste any further time in argument but
simply threw the weapons into the river.

The Christian king gave the visitors a most
friendly welcome and talked to them about the
Gospel. The palaver was a great success. Trade
began between the two tribes and Mary's influence was increased yet more. Rapidly she was
earning the title of "White Queen of Okoyong"
by which she has been so often described.

VI

AMONG AFRICA'S CHILDREN

AFTER three years at Okoyong, Mary was due for
another holiday at home. Fever had laid her low
once again, but she did not want to leave the
work until there was someone to take over and

keep an eye on things. She knew only too well how easily these people would slip back into their heathen ways if left on their own again. Then all that had been achieved would be undone and the work would have to start all over again.

Fortunately a Miss Dunlop reached the station to take Mary's place, but just as she was leaving news was received that a young man had been wounded in a shooting affray. She could not go knowing that she alone, with God's help, could prevent the bloodshed that would probably result. She hurried after the avengers and overtook them just as they were preparing an attack on another village. She pleaded with them to turn back and, during the silence which followed her little speech, she pleaded with God to turn their hearts from evil. Her prayer was answered and the dusky warriors promised that while she was away they would forget their quarrels and live peaceably. With this promise to encourage her, she set off on her long journey from Ekenge to Dundee.

Early in 1891 Mary reached England on her third furlough. This time there was no mother to visit in Dundee. Indeed she had no near relatives left. Accordingly she went first, not to Scotland, but to Devon to visit those who had cared for her mother and last surviving sister in the months preceding their deaths. Here she enjoyed a well-deserved rest amid beautiful surroundings in what is probably the most pleasant climate in the British Isles.

Once she was thoroughly rested people expected

her to go to their churches to speak about her work. In Africa she had faced death and danger with calmness and courage. At home she was shy and reluctant to speak about her work lest people should think she was boasting. Sometimes those who went to hear her were disappointed because she preached the Gospel to them instead of telling them of its triumphs in Africa. When she did tell of these triumphs her audiences listened spellbound and great interest was aroused in the work of missions everywhere.

When an attack of bronchitis made it impossible for her to go about speaking at meetings, she wrote a number of articles which were published in a missionary magazine in which among other things she said how important it was that natives should be taught trades such as carpentry or furniture making. This was altogether a new idea to those who were responsible for running missionary work. It would mean sending to the mission field tradesmen as well as missionaries. Eventually it was decided to do something along the lines that Mary had suggested and a Training Institute was founded for the purpose. It was named after Hope Waddell, the missionary who started the work in Calabar two years before Mary Slessor was born.

Early in 1892 Mary returned to Calabar. When she reached Okoyong she found not only that the buildings had been enlarged and improved but that real progress was being made in that the natives were gradually giving up their dreadful customs. Thus, in her absence God had continued the good work through someone else.

Not that all their customs were evil, however. There were some, particularly those connected with children, which were very much to the contrary. For instance, as soon as a little girl was able to walk to the fountain and fill a pot with water, she was encouraged to visit everyone in the village and to give each one a little of her water. They, in return, would give her some small present.

In the case of little boys, as soon as they learned to shoot, they would take their first trophy to the local chief-who would pay him some money for it or give him a palm-wine tree. When a boy first climbed an oil-palm tree it was the custom for him to give the first bunch of nuts he obtained to his father and the second to his mother.

Each year a children's festival was held at the time of the yam harvest. When the people were taking their yams and other produce to market, the children would stand beside the path and ask for a small gift. Most people would hand them something, usually eatable, though it might be only a snail—which is regarded in many countries as something very delicious—and all the gifts were cooked together in a king of stew which the children would eat and apparently enjoy!

As we already know there were many customs not so pleasant as these. At a very early age a child was trained to take a gift to the local god or juju, who was supposed to be the guardian of the

village in which he lived. Thus early in life did
he begin to believe in the superstitions which came
to have such a dreadful hold on him as he grew up.

We have mentioned the terrible belief about
twins. Equally cruel was the attitude to babies
whose mothers died. Usually these were thrown
away into the bush or just left alone to die. Sometimes a woman might be willing to bring the baby
up, but she would be afraid of the jealousy of the
dead mother and would end up by doing nothing.
Such children as these Mary Slessor rescued
whenever possible.

One day some women who had been to market
casually mentioned to her that on their way back
they had heard a baby crying in the bush, re-
marking how extraordinary it was that a baby
should still be alive after five days and nights in
the open. They had simply passed by like the two
men in our Lord's story of the Good Samaritan.
Mary made them tell her just where the baby was
and then she ran off as fast as she possibly could
to rescue it. It was amazing that it was still alive,
for, not only had it been there nearly a week,
but it had been attacked by white ants. Wonderful to relate the baby survived and grew into a
healthy, happy child, named Mary after her
rescuer and foster mother.

At any hour of the day or night Mary Slessor
would journey forth to rescue new-born twins.
Her friend, Ma Eme, would send her a message
whenever she heard of a case. Then Mary would
not delay for a moment. She would set off for the

village where the twins had been born. Often she would arrive to find that the babies had been already killed or so ill treated that there was little hope of keeping them alive; but sometimes she would be in time to save their lives and bring them back to her own home. Even then her difficulties were not over. Those of you who have or have had baby brothers or sisters know how often a baby cries out for something and can only be calmed into quietness again by its mother. Fortunately negro babies do not cry as much as white babies, but Mary had no easy task in finding suitable food for them. More than once she tramped for hours through the forest to Creek Town to obtain milk or other food. Often she would be kept awake at night by a baby that was ill or in pain and for whom she could do little. The babies slept in hammocks fixed between Mary's bed and the walls of the room. To each hammock was fastened a cord which was within her reach. When a child awoke and was crying, she would pull on the cord; this would set the hammock rocking and often lull the child to sleep again.

Sometimes, of course, the babies died in spite of all that she did for them. On one occasion four of her rescued babies died within a month. This would make her very sad and the people would be most impressed to realise how much she cared for these helpless bundles of humanity.

With so many to look after and so much else to do, she had to find native girls to help her and these were not always as careful with the babies as Mary herself would be. There was one little rescued twin, a girl called Susie, who had survived though her brother had died, when both had been crammed into a small box and the mother turned out into the bush. This child was of such a light colour that she looked almost like a white baby. Mary was particularly fond of her and had named her after one of her sisters. One day, while the missionary was away from home, Susie was accidentally scalded through the carelessness of a native girl looking after her and died from the effects of the burns.

Sometimes Mary would find that the parents of twins were willing to keep the babies but were afraid of what the tribe would say and do. The wife of a young chief had twins in a village some distance from Mary's home. The parents had heard the Gospel from Mary and longed to give up their heathen ways, but were afraid of their neighbours. They, therefore, sent to Mary to come and take their babies. Unfortunately one of the babies died before the two girls sent by the missionary arrived, but the other was brought back safely to the Mission. Not long afterwards the parents came to see the child which they were afraid to rear themselves. For a time they stayed nearby and listened carefully as Mary explained Christ's teaching to them. Next she sent for the leading men of the tribe and preached the Gospel to them also, telling them that God had sent her to teach them to give up their old customs and to permit twins and their mothers to live normal lives. The men listened to all she had to say very politely, but it was clear that they did not like the idea of giving up this particular custom. Mary next went to the village and held a service in the home of the young chief, after which she distributed presents to each of his wives. The young man made his decision for Christ and showed that he meant it by casting out of his house all the sacred ornaments used in connection with the heathen worship.

Mary Slessor was always ready to go out on a tedious or dangerous journey in order to help those who needed her or to prevent outbreaks of trouble. The native chiefs did not know that Ma Eme was in the habit of letting her know where her presence was needed and could not understand how the white woman knew so much about them and their plans. They were duly impressed and put it down to some kind of magic.

A journey through the African bush before the making of roads was not a pleasant experience for anyone. For this lonely Scottish woman it must have been very trying indeed; but never did she show any signs of fear. Wild beasts might be prowling around and she might hear their weird noises, but she would think of Daniel, whose God shut the mouths of lions and to that same God she would pray, "O God of Daniel, shut their mouths."

If she was afraid that trouble might start before she could arrive to prevent it, she would send a runner ahead of her carrying a large sheet of paper on which she had written a few words and symbols. The "message" would be quite meaningless and in any case the people to whom she sent it would be unable to read, but they would study it carefully and try to work out the puzzle. More often than not the delay caused by the "letter" would be long enough to allow Mary to reach the scene of trouble.

Sometimes she would attend a native palaver or discussion. She would sit quietly knitting under a brightly coloured umbrella, while chiefs, surrounded by armed and bloodthirsty warriors, would argue for hours on end. Mary would listen carefully. When she had heard enough, she would give her opinion, and so highly did they think of her that usually they would accept her solution to the argument. Thus did she become a kind of unofficial judge, to whom they turned for advice whenever there were matters in dispute.

In 1889 the native tribes of Nigeria agreed to accept the protection of the British Government. An area known as the Niger Coast Protectorate came into existence. The first consul to be appointed was a gentleman named Sir Claude MacDonald. He wanted to send a vice-consul to look after British interests in the Okoyong district, but when he discovered what great influence Mary Slessor had over the tribes in that area he decided that she should be the vice-consul there. This was the first time in the history of the British Empire that a woman had received such an appointment.

Knowing that the tribes would not allow strangers to come among them, laying down new laws and settling their disputes, Mary asked for official permission to do this herself. Permission was readily given and the quiet Scottish woman became a most successful magistrate. She used the authority given to her to promote laws which would improve the lot of the poorer natives and administered justice throughout the area. The British Government was amazed at the way she could handle these uncivilised natives. She showed rare skill in solving the many problems which were brought to her, but she sought daily guidance from Him of whom it has been said, "If any of you lack wisdom, let him ask of God . . . and it shall be given him."

Mary Slessor was anxious that these other activities should not interfere with her first and most important task—the spreading of the Gospel. The fact that she was officially recognised by the authorities was in many ways a great help. It meant that she could easily obtain permits to travel on roads and rivers and that she could get her house repaired without having to send for a mission worker.

In common with many people who have great faith in God, Mary did not take the normal precautions against malaria and other tropical diseases. She would not sleep under a mosquito net or take quinine regularly or make sure that all her water had been filtered before she drank it. It was believed by white people at that time that to go out in the sun without a hat was asking for trouble. Mary's friends knew that she did not like to wear a hat and one of them wrote to her saying that it was her vanity that made her want to let people see her pretty hair! But she took little notice of such well meant advice.

When she had first gone to live in the bush, she had made up her mind to live as nearly like the natives as possible. This meant that she lived more cheaply so that she was able to send money to her mother; also she felt that she would have greater influence over the natives than if she lived as one apart. Thus she trained herself to eat native food and to walk barefoot through the bush. She did not, of course, dress like the natives, though her clothes were always very simple and suitable for what she was doing. She did most of her own repairs and whitewashed her walls when necessary. When writing about the sort of missionaries who were needed in the bush, Mary would emphasise the practical side—knowledge of how to nurse a baby, and how to bring up children, was almost as important as knowledge of the Scriptures if the missionary was to do a really useful work.

One of her problems concerned the two great ceremonies—sacraments they are often called—connected with Christianity, baptism and Holy Communion. In the branch of the Church to which Mary belonged it was necessary for an ordained minister to perform these. As no ministers were available, Mary felt that these cere-

monies could not be held. Her task was to preach
the Gospel and this she did whenever opportunity
offered. Her reward was to see the changed lives
and habits of these dark-skinned savages for whom
Christ had died. Within a few years of her going to
Okoyong she was able to report that raiding,
plundering and the stealing of slaves had almost
entirely ceased; that the custom of sacrificing
human victims on the death of a chief had died
out; and that the killing of twins and motherless
babies had ended. Even the natives themselves
were amazed at what she accomplished. "Ma,"
said one chief to her, "you white people are God
Almighty; no other power could have done this."
There was less heavy drinking, especially among
women, and a genuine desire for education.

The organisation of schools, however, presented
the missionary with many problems. To begin
with, most of the children were afraid to travel
through the bush to school because of evil spirits.
They seemed to be more afraid of them than of
the wild animals which were a real danger.
Then boys would often be kept away from school
to take part in tribal customs, while girls would
be kept away so that they could be fattened up in
preparation for marriage. Mary herself had far
too many other things to do to devote much time
to teaching and in letters home she urged that
teachers be sent out for the purpose.

She had many friends at home who from time
to time sent her large parcels, containing sweets,
clothes, books, pictures and anything else they

could think of, for Mary had told them that almost everything could be of use if only to attract the interest of the natives in something they had never seen before. There was great excitement whenever one of these parcels arrived. The children would crowd around as the contents were unpacked. This was usually done on the landing beach, as the complete parcels were too large and heavy to carry easily through the narrow bush path. Mary was very fond of home-made toffee and most of the parcels contained a tin of this which was shared out among as many as possible. Sometimes people would send her dolls, but she would not give these away as she was afraid some of the natives would try to worship them. Instead she kept them for sewing lessons, using them to show how clothes were made and worn.

In the African bush it is not very often that one receives visitors, but Mary received a most interesting visitor on one occasion. Her name was Mary Kingsley and she was a niece of Charles Kingsley, who wrote *The Water Babies, Westward Ho!* and other famous books. This lady was not a Christian but she was deeply interested in the welfare of primitive peoples and she loved to travel in strange and dangerous places. She had heard so much about the wonderful work Mary Slessor was doing that she went to Ekenge to see for herself. She was most impressed with the work when she saw it and took a great liking to the missionary with her family of rescued babies. Her testimony is particularly interesting because she did not believe that Christianity should be taught to the natives. Of Mary Slessor she wrote: "The amount of good she has done no man can fully estimate." She looked upon her as the ideal of what a white woman should be, ruling a primitive tribe.

Mary Kingsley wrote a most interesting account of her experiences under the title *Travels in West Africa*. A few years after the visit to Ekenge she was nursing prisoners during the Boer War, when she caught a fever and died at the age of thirty-eight.

VII

ON INTO THE BUSH

In 1896 Mary decided that for the benefit of the work she ought to move to Akpap, a market town several miles south of Ekenge. Her reason lay in the African way of life which causes the natives to move on to fresh scenes from time to time. They have learned from long experience that crops grow best on soil which has been unused for a long time. Their homes being simple affairs, easily, quickly and cheaply built, they desert their huts and build a fresh village near to the land which they intend to cultivate. When the time came for the people of Ekenge to make such a move Mary decided to go with them so that she could follow up the work which had been begun. There was another advantage. The move would bring her within reach of other villages where the

Gospel had never been preached. At first the Board responsible for the running of the Mission did not like Mary's idea, partly because a new house would have to be built for the missionary and partly because Akpap was six miles from the landing beach, along a trail which would be very difficult to follow. After a time, however, the Board gave in to Mary and promised to build a mission house in Akpap. But Mary could not wait until it was possible to send skilled men for the work. She obtained a two-roomed native shed and turned it into a home for herself, very primitive but good enough to use until a more permanent building was ready. The shed had no windows and was already fully occupied with lizards, rats, mice and other animals!

When one of the missionaries did come to Akpap to help with the building, he went into Mary's shed to have a wash. In the water he found what he thought was a sponge. He was surprised that Mary should have one but used it while washing. Afterwards he discovered that the "sponge" was really a drowned rat.

Not long after her move to Akpap there was an epidemic of smallpox in the district. In England we do not often hear of smallpox now, but that is only because most of us have been vaccinated. Among the African natives, of course, vaccination was unknown, but Mary had a supply of vaccine, the fluid of which is injected into the bloodstream to prevent the disease. As long as her supply of the precious fluid lasted she vaccinated the natives and no doubt her action saved many lives. When all the vaccine had been used up she used blood from those who had received an injection. The house in which she had lived at Ekenge she turned into a hospital, where she tended the victims, many of whom died, among them Chief Edem himself. Alone at the time, Mary made a coffin with her own hands, reverently placed the chief's body inside it and buried it in a grave she had dug herself. She was sad at his death. Though he had never professed to become a Christian, he had often proved himself a true friend and had said that he knew the ways of heathenism were wrong. Mary quietly committed him to God who knows the hearts of all men, and rejoiced that for the first time in the history of the village a chief had been buried without the killing of wives and slaves and prisoners.

So many died of the smallpox that at one time the house at Ekenge was filled with dead bodies. Fortunately two missionaries from Duke Town came to visit Mary about this time; they helped to clear the house, after which it was never used again.

In spite of all this extra work, Mary kept her other activities going. Each evening her little family of rescued twins would gather with the patients to hear Mary read the Scriptures and commit them all to God's care. Often they joined in the singing of a hymn, usually to a Scottish air, with the missionary accompanying on a tambourine. If someone grew weary and nodded off to sleep, Mary would attract their attention with a light tap with her instrument.

The long hours spent nursing the sick were a great strain on Mary. She had had no holiday at home for several years and now was an excellent opportunity while Mr. Ovens was building the new mission at Akpap and would be able to keep an eye on things during her absence. Her main anxiety concerned the children. She did not want to leave them to the mercy of natives and did not like to ask other missionaries to do what she felt was her work. Finally, however, homes were found for all except four girls, whom she decided to take to Scotland with her. The eldest of these was Janie, now sixteen, while the other three were all under five, the youngest being only sixteen months. In those days few people from Africa had ever been seen in England or Scotland and we can imagine the interest aroused by the sight of the missionary with her four dark-skinned children. She tried not to take them about too much in public because people were very rude and used to stare at them. It is interesting to note that at the time of this visit to her homeland she had rescued from death no fewer than fifty-one twins.

The first few weeks of her furlough were spent resting at a place called Bowden; then, as soon as she felt strong enough, she went round the churches telling Christians at home what God was doing in Calabar and pleading for more workers. Speaking in public was never easy for her; it was even more difficult now that she spoke her mother tongue so rarely. Wherever she went, however, people were deeply stirred and interest was aroused in the work of the missionaries.

During the years since her previous visit a new invention had appeared on the roads—the motor car. Coming from her primitive surroundings in Africa, Mary found the roads of big cities like Edinburgh and Glasgow quite alarming. Often she was afraid to cross unless someone was with her. This little fact reminds us again that the courage with which she faced the most hair-raising situations in the African bush was given her by the God she served. When doing His work, she never knew fear in any shape of form.

The new house at Akpap was much better than her old one at Ekenge had been. Mr. Ovens worked hard while Mary was away. The house had two floors, with an outside staircase, a balcony and a verandah. Mary soon settled down to her life of endless activity again, only regretting that her health was not as good as it had been twenty years before. She visited the villages around Akpap, tending the sick and preaching the Gospel. Many a native who lived in some remote spot testified that the "White Ma" had told him about Jesus. So famous did she become that it was not unknown for natives to travel many miles in order to see her.

An insight into her daily life has been given us by a missionary who visited her about this time.

With her lived twelve rescued children, six little boys, four little girls and two bigger girls. At six o'clock every morning Mary would set off through the bush to a village three miles away where she would take school. In the afternoon she would be back at Akpap for school there. Surgery time was after tea. Every fourth day was an extra busy one, when large numbers of natives came into the town for market. To her they brought all their troubles. On Sundays she visited several villages to hold services. So busy was she that sometimes she forgot which day of the week it was. Once she was found holding her Sunday services on a Monday and on another occasion was repairing her roof on a Sunday thinking it was a Monday.

About this time six young men professed faith in Christ and after being trained by Mary went out to surrounding villages to spread the Gospel. Mary was still not too old to go on exploration trips far into the bush. Often she would travel either in a canoe or a launch on these journeys. Once her launch was attacked by a hippopotamus but she fought the beast off with her cooking utensils!

Meanwhile Nigeria was undergoing important changes. For purposes of government the country was divided into two parts. Southern Nigeria was particularly difficult to bring under control and a tribe called the Aros caused the authorities a great deal of trouble. These Aros offered human sacrifices, were cannibals, and made constant war against more peaceful tribes. Mary realised that above all else they needed a change of heart which could only come when they had learned the way of Christ and had received Him into their hearts. She was greatly saddened, therefore, when the Government sent a military expedition against them. Fearing trouble up-country, Government officials were afraid that Mary might not be safe. Accordingly they said she would have to go back to the coast for a time.

She was very upset at having to leave her people, knowing that war might break out among the tribes, in which many of her coloured friends might be killed. She was unwell at the time and found the sky away from the dark forests "terribly bright." But the people of Okoyong showed how greatly they had taken her to their hearts by sending regular gifts to their "queen" as they called her.

Someone who knew her during the time she was down at the coast, waiting for the trouble to blow over, has written an interesting description of her: "She is usually found bareheaded and and barefooted. A twin baby is most likely to be in her arms and a swarm of children about her . . . She is always busy." Another one wrote: "I never saw anything more beautiful than her devotion to these black children. She had a sick boy in her arms the whole time I was there. She carried him about, caring for his needs, all the while directing the other work to be done."

As soon as affairs up-country had calmed down, Mary returned to Akpap, where, in 1902, she was

joined by another missionary, a Miss Wright. For
fourteen years she had been the only white woman
among hordes of savages. Now she had company.
The two soon became firm friends and got on very
well together. "Things go on as smoothly as on a
summer's day," wrote Mary, "and I don't know
however I got on alone."

In the following year, Mary had the joy of
seeing the first Christian church in Okoyong
firmly established. A number of converts were
baptised and a Communion service was held at
which native Christians and the missionaries
broke bread together and drank the wine which
serves as a constant reminder to Christians of the
love of Christ in shedding His blood and allowing
His body to be broken for them. Mary wept tears
of joy as she saw the fulfilment of all that she had
lived for and worked for since her coming to
Africa. In a moving address to the Christian
natives she reminded them of the great changes
which Christ's power had worked in their lives
and told them that all who had not become
Christians would be watching them. If they
remained true to Christ, that would be proof of
the power of the Gospel.

Needless to say, as soon as Miss Wright had
settled down to the work, Mary started planning
fresh conquests for Christ. She explored up the
river as far as a place called Arochuko which was
in the heart of the country occupied by Aros and a
centre for the buying and selling of slaves. Next
she took with her two of the young Christians and

left them to start schools for children in two villages hitherto untouched.

In each village she visited she persuaded the people to build a place for the worship of the true God. Sometimes it would only be a small hut or shed, but a true Christian church was being established in the midst of heathenism. The people were beginning to awake from centuries of ignorance and evil and to thirst after the truth. On one of her journeys she lost her way and met two men who asked her eagerly if she had come with God's Word.

"What else should I come with?" she replied.

"Oh," they answered, "we have built a small church and we are longing for you to come and teach us, and we will build a house for you to come and stay in." She was not able to go to their village then, but promised to do so at the first opportunity. On the same journey she met a man, travelling with his wives and other relatives, who had been far westwards across country until he had come to the great River Niger. There he had heard the Gospel preached and was longing for someone to tell him more.

It was laid down by the British authorities that all land obtained from natives had to be paid for and registered. Yet, so anxious were many villages to have a church and a school that they would gladly have given land for the purpose. In one place an offer of £2 10s. 0d. was refused, the chief accepting no more than a shilling and that only in order to comply with the regulations.

VIII

ONWARD TO THE CANNIBALS

THE area to which Mary Slessor was now wanting to carry the Good News was one which had been avoided both by traders and missionaries because of the fierce nature of the tribes. Deep in the forest, away from the river lived the Ibo tribe which was dominated by the Aros who had been giving the Government so much trouble. These Aros lived at a place called Arochuko. Their religion was known as juju worship, the jujus being spells or magic charms. The juju might take a fairly harmless form, such as a heap of yams or a bundle of firewood tied round with a grass rope and with a large knot at the top. It would mean that the crop growing there had been committed to the care of a spirit who would cause some dreadful accident to happen to anyone who tried to steal the crop. So strong is the belief in this kind of juju even today that no one will dare to touch any crop or property so protected.

In Mary Slessor's time juju worship held the tribes completely under the power of the jujuman or witch doctor. Their religion provided them with slaves and if there was any shortage of slaves the Aros would attack a village and carry away as many natives as they wanted. Each village had its juju tree in which the juju god was supposed to live. Such trees were sacred and were looked after by the jujumen, who were very powerful in the tribe.

It happened sometimes that a juju would gain more than local importance. An outstanding example of this was what was known as the Long Juju, about a mile from Arochuko. It consisted of a kind of shrine in a cave on an island in the middle of a lake. The only way to it was by a winding path through dense bush. To this place came natives from surrounding villages to worship their god and to consult the jujumen. A terrible fate awaited them, for few ever returned to their villages. They were captured on arrival and sold into slavery. Sometimes they were offered as human sacrifices and sometimes they were eaten, for the Aros were cannibals. It was not unusual for a whole village, men, women and children, to come on pilgrimage to the Long Juju, little knowing that as they journeyed on that last fearful mile from Arochuko to the shrine they would be set upon, killed and eaten, or captured to spend the rest of their lives in slavery.

The British authorities eventually put an end to the dreadful atrocities committed there by blowing up the cave and setting free the slaves who were there; but when Mary Slessor first explored this part of Africa, she planned to take the Gospel of God's love to these cruel tribesmen and the thousands of natives who were being ruthlessly killed and enslaved. She would, had she been allowed, have gone with one of the military expeditions sent from time to time by

the British Government to keep law and order.
If she heard of a trader who was going among the
people, she would tell him to say that she intended
to go there herself to live as soon as arrangements
could be made. It was not an attractive prospect,
but Mary believed that the God who had worked
wonders among the Okoyong tribe could and
would work wonders among the Ibos and Aros.
She was horrified to hear of the needless slaughter
of human beings. For instance, when a chief died,
as many as fifty or more natives would be killed
and eaten, in addition to the beheading of some
two dozen others as part of the burial ceremonies.

Another tribe to whom she was anxious to
preach the Gospel was the Ibibios, an extremely
degraded people, living in constant fear of the
Aros in a part of the bush most difficult to reach.
She was overjoyed when an opportunity arose to
send the Good News ahead of her. A Government
official came back to Nigeria from a furlough in
England with a gramophone and some records of
well-known hymns, such as "Abide with me."
These records, together with lantern slides,
astonished the natives, who had never imagined
anything so wonderful. The official also had a
machine on which Mary could record a message
and she spoke into it in the native tongue the
wonderful story of the Prodigal Son, told in Luke
15. The official was going out among the Ibibios
and he took the gramophone with him, to play the
Gospel message in every village. Mary was thrilled
that what was then a new invention should be

thus used in Christ's service. She saw wonderful possibilities if wealthy Christians would come forward to help. "A person with means," she remarked, "could have the Gospel carried round like that when unable to speak a word of the language."

Mary Slessor was particularly fond of the lovely story of the Prodigal Son which she had recorded, also of the other two parables contained in Luke 15, the parables of the lost sheep and the lost coin. As she went from place to place, visiting towns and villages, she repeated these stories again and again. Once, after she had told the story of the lost sheep, a tall native came out and in front of all the people of his town, said, "I shall pray and try and if God will only put me on His shoulder and bring me out of the bush—well, we shall see!"

Sometimes she heard of people in this region who were actually asking for the Gospel to be preached to them. A chief, who lived on the shore of Enyong Creek, a scene of extraordinary natural beauty in the very heart of heathenism, was visited by Mary. She found him to be "a soul in darkness, wrestling towards God and light and peace." To her surprise he produced a Bible and hymn book. They had belonged to a son, who had died, who had been in contact with missionaries and had learned to love the things of God.

The following Sunday he sent a canoe for her. When she arrived to take a service, a bell was being run to call the people together. Some of

them could even say the Lord's Prayer and
repeat a hymn and some portions of Scrip-
ture.

Near the mouth of the creek was a town called
Itu. For many years, longer than anyone could
remember, this town had been a centre of the
slave trade. From Itu countless slaves had been
shipped to the West Indies and the American
colonies. When Mary first went there she saw the
huts in which victims of slave raids were im-
prisoned, posts to which they were chained while
awaiting sale, and platforms from which the
wicked trade was conducted. This town she chose
as a suitable centre for work among the Ibibios,
although her Mission wanted a base further up
the river. Knowing what she did of the climate,
weather conditions and difficulties of travelling,
she insisted that Itu was the most suitable place.
This was finally agreed to and Mary went there
with plans to open stations at Arochuko and a
place called Bende as soon as possible.

By this time there had been enough converts
trained to do evangelistic work themselves for
Mary to use some of them in pioneer work. She
accordingly started the work at Itu and then left
it in the hands of native evangelists while she
returned for a time to Akpap. When she was able
to get back to Itu, she found to her joy that a fine
work was being done by these natives and that
they were ready to begin building a church. This
was duly carried out, Mary working on the
building with her own hands—and she was nearly

sixty now. Two rooms were built on as living quarters for herself and another missionary. A school also was built so that the natives could learn to read and write.

For a time she continued to journey backwards and forwards between Itu and Akpap, keeping a motherly eye on converts and watching the growing Christian influence in the two areas. On one of her journeys she met a Colonel Montanara, who knew of her desire to reach the troublesome Aros and offered her the protection of his forces to go to Arochuko. Once there, she walked through the dense bush where so many had taken their last steps in life or in freedom to the lake where the Long Juju was. Around her she saw the skulls and bones of those who had been slaughtered and the cooking pots in which victims had been roasted for eating. As the appalling evidence impressed upon her the tragic state of those who for long centuries had lived their miserable existence without Christ, she prayed that here, as in Okoyong, God would cause the light of His glorious Gospel to shine. Surprisingly she found the people quite friendly. They had heard of her work elsewhere and knew of her great courage and goodness. She promised that as soon as possible she would be back among them to start a school. In spite of the fact that the authorities would not give permission for a station to be opened at Arochuko, Mary took a small party of native Christians to a nearby village called Amasa and here a school was opened. At once

young people, both boys and girls, crowded
into it "thirsty for the Book and the loving
God."

Returning to Akpap, full of joy at this beginning
of Christian witness in the midst of juju worship,
her canoe was waylaid by another canoe occupied
by a native who handed her a letter. Amazed
to receive a message in writing from an African,
Mary ordered her men to follow the canoe. They
were led to a very beautiful spot on the shore of
the creek, where they were met by a young native
chief and his wife. The man's name was Onoyom
Iya Nya and he was a man of some influence,
being president of the local native court. Then he
told her his story. He had as a boy travelled with
a missionary, acting as a guide. He had heard the
Gospel and had been most impressed, but when he
he spoke of it among his people he had been cruelly
treated. In consequence he had taken the easiest
course and had followed the heathen customs of
his people, even to taking part in the terrible
cannibal feasts. Yet at the back of his mind was
the knowledge of what he had heard, like a seed
which has fallen into poor soil where it does not
die and yet cannot grow. In his desire really to
know the way of God, he spoke to others of his
longing and met someone who put it into his head
that maybe the "God of the white man" was
angry with him. "How can I find this God?"
asked Onoyom. "I am not worthy to say," was the
reply, "but find the White Ma who goes to Itu
and she will tell you." Thus he had sent one of his

servants to wait for Mary's canoe as she came
down the river.

The new stations were very successful. In
Amaso many were learning to read and a church
was built at Itu in which large numbers gathered
to worship the true God, also a house for the
missionary with no fewer than six rooms. Mary
protested at the size of the house, but the natives
assured her that nothing was too much trouble
and continued with their work. She next decided
to make Itu her main base, from where she would
go on expeditions to carry the Gospel to the many
villages where the name of Christ had never been
heard. So strongly did she feel the need of these
savage cannibals that she was prepared to give up
her furlough in Britain in order to spend the time
exploring the area and planning its evangelisation.

At about this time some money was given to
the Mission by a friend in Scotland for the building of a hospital at Itu. A condition was that the
hospital should be called the Mary Slessor
Memorial Hospital. A South African doctor was
appointed to take charge and the hospital became
a wonderful centre of healing and evangelism.

The country was now being developed by the
Government. Roads and railways were being
built and natives from villages far and near came
to work on them. Mary at once seized the opportunity to preach the Gospel to them, praying that
they would carry the message back to their homes.
So great was the confidence placed in her by white
officials and by African chiefs that her advice was

constantly sought. The officials would ask her about native customs, while the chiefs were anxious to know whether the changes taking place would be for the good of their people.

Though getting on for sixty, she learned to ride a bicycle. She learned easily and was delighted that it enabled her to get about more quickly.

Mary was particularly anxious to do something to help the womenfolk of this new area. Worst off were the unmarried who were treated little better than slaves. Often girls came to her who had fled from some place where they were cruelly treated. She felt strongly that God was calling her to organise a school for them where they could be taught to read and write and also a craft or trade. So sure was she that God was leading her in these new ventures that she was prepared if necessary to break the connection with her Mission if anyone tried to prevent her from going ahead with her plans. She even considered the possibility of opening a store, so that she could be independent and free to go where she felt led. During the period she was exploring she was on a special leave and was paying all her own expenses. As she saw the road being extended into the bush, she felt that she just had to go on. She realised that she was not so strong as in her younger days, but calmly talked of getting a little cart made from some wheels and an old box in which she could ride pulled by her children!

However, when the Mission saw how certain she was of God's leading and how determined to open up new work, they agreed to her proposals. A missionary named John Rankin was sent to the area to study the situation. When he visited Arochuko, he found that within three miles were nineteen other villages, most of which were trying to change their ways and were asking for teachers. One who was ready to turn his back on heathen customs was the chief of the Aros, the man mainly responsible for the atrocities carried on in connection with the Long Juju.

IX

MARY THE MAGISTRATE

MR. RANKIN was appointed by the Mission to look after the new work at Arochuko and Itu, while Mary was able to press on to the unreached tribes further up the river. For some time she had not been accepting any salary from the Mission, but she was never a rich woman and could not go on doing that much longer. Now, however, something happened which set her free from worries about money. She was asked by the Government to act as the local magistrate, in which position she had the opportunity to see more of the people and to help the most degraded. Her heart was deeply moved by what she saw. Before her came men and women accused of murder, attempted suicide, cruelty and violence. She received some help from local chiefs and a jury, but she had to make all the important decisions herself. This new work gave her a chance to do something for twins and she proved a most successful magistrate. One official reported: "She combines most happily kindliness and severity and I cannot imagine any native trying to take advantage of her kindness and her great-hearted love for the people."

Her court work, together with her untiring efforts in evangelism were a great strain on her health. In 1906 she was told by a doctor that she must go back to Scotland for a furlough. So much did she love the work that she hated to leave it and kept going as long as possible, but in 1907, her fifty-ninth year, she had to give in. She was so weak that she had to be carried from place to place. She returned to her homeland for the last time.

She needed a long rest in order to recover her health and strength. In the home of some old friends who lived near Edinburgh she found a happy and peaceful retreat. She still did unusual things as she had done all her life. Often, instead of sitting on a chair, she would lie full length on the hearth rug, telling her friends stories of Calabar. Breakfast was taken up to her bedroom and afterwards they would sit at her bedside while she read to them favourite passages from her well-worn Bible.

Wherever she went people welcomed her most warmly. She was now a famous woman. Those who heard her speak were thrilled to hear the stirring account of what God was doing among the heathen. Her only worry while at home was that harm might come to her rescued twins. She feared that while she was away they might slip back into heathen ways. She was anxious to get back because so much remained to be done. She longed to see laws passed which would grant protection to women, especially the unmarried and widows.

And so, in October 1907, Mary Slessor left Scotland for the last time. The rest of her days, apart from a holiday in the Canary Islands, were to be spent in her adopted land.

On arrival in Calabar she went inland to a place called Okotobong and settled down to work harder than ever before—teaching, dispensing medicine, presiding over court cases and at all times spreading the Good News. On Sundays she would visit as many as a dozen villages holding services in each.

She now had the joy of seeing the fruits of her earlier work. One memorable day, soon after her return, a baptismal and communion service was held. Great crowds gathered and Mary remembered that only four years before, there had not been one single Christian in this place. Now there were many and they were giving generously for the spreading of the Gospel among other tribes.

Still she longed to push on to those who were unreached. About twenty miles up the Enyong Creek, a tributary of the Cross River, was yet another important centre of the slave trade called Ikpe. Natives from Ikpe sent to her saying that they too wanted to become "God-men." It took her two days to get there by canoe, but when she did so she saw at once that it was an ideal place from which to work in order to reach many more who were still floundering in the darkness of heathenism. Though not yet Christians, the natives were so keen for a missionary to live among them that they had started to build a small church and house. In the partly-built church she preached the Gospel to a great crowd who had never heard it before. She was sure that God wanted her to move to Ikpe, but for a time it was not to be. She was again suffering ill effects from trying to work too hard. In 1909 she had to give up her work as a magistrate, and soon afterwards she was fetched in the official Government car and taken to the hospital at Itu which had been named in her honour. When well enough to leave there, she went to Duke Town on the coast, where kind friends nursed her back to health and strength. As soon as she was well enough she went inland again. From Ikotobong she cycled fifteen miles to a place called Ikot Ekpene, choosing sites for schools and churches in the villages through which she passed.

Meanwhile she did not forget Ikpe. News from there was that a group of natives were meeting together, though they knew but little of Christianity. A native teacher was with them, passing on what he knew, but that was not much. Mary was so anxious to do something that she was willing to give up the small salary she was again receiving if it could be used to send a worker there. She thought she could live very cheaply on native food.

But at last the way opened for her to go to Ikpe herself. She moved into the house prepared. It was a nice place, set amid stately palm trees, but too near the water where the malaria-carrying mosquitoes lurked. Often she made the journey by canoe back to Ikot Obong to make sure that all was going well there. When the house was struck by a tornado she repaired it herself with her own hands. Sometimes she was too tired even to undress before she went to bed. The Mission doctor ordered her to rest more and forbade her to use her bicycle, but he found her a very difficult patient. There was so much to be done and so few willing to do it. Again and again she was laid low with fever. She hated having to go into hospital, for it kept her away from the work she loved. We can guess something of her feelings at this time by reading some of the things she said about herself. In letters she called herself "a broken reed" and "a sputtering candle." She said that her wrinkles were like a "wonderfully folded concertina." To her great disappointment no worker was sent to Ikpe in her place, because doctors reported that it was too unhealthy.

Some friends at home, hearing of her weakness and of her determination to carry on as long as life was in her, sent her a small cart which could be wheeled along by two natives. She dare not leave the work to come home for another furlough,

fearing that if she did so no one would be available
to carry on and all her efforts would be wasted.
It was remarkable that she was still alive. A doctor
told her that anyone else would have been dead
long before.

At last she was persuaded to have a holiday. It
was pointed out to her that her life and health
were of real importance to the young church in
the bush villages where she had spent thirty-six
years. At first she considered a holiday an extra-
vagant luxury, but when she realised that it was
the only way in which she was likely to regain
strength to do still more work for her Master, she
gave in. Thus, in 1912, she sailed from Calabar
to the lovely climate of the Canary Islands,
praying that He who had healed the sick in
Galilee nineteen centuries before would give
health and strength to her weak body to enable
her to work a little longer for Him.

The Canary Islands lie far out in the Atlantic,
over 200 miles from the coast of North Africa.
There are seven of them on which people live,
the largest being called Grand Canary. This was
the last land Columbus saw before he crossed the
Atlantic to discover the New World. It is one of
the world's most famed beauty spots, with magni-
ficent tropical flowers and plants and superb views
of valleys and the sea. Here Mary Slessor spent a
memorable holiday. Amid so much beauty she
felt the nearness of God, the Creator of it all. In
her hotel she met people who professed not to
believe in sending missionaries to the heathen.

Many of them changed their attitude when Mary told them about Calabar. Her health and strength returned. A doctor examined her and told her she would probably be able to carry on for many years—*if she was careful*. But Mary just could not be careful! She was not made that way. While she had the strength she just had to use it fully.

X

MARY'S REWARD

AFTER this holiday in the Canary Islands, she went back refreshed and ready for fresh advances. During the next two years she travelled a good deal, dividing her time between Ikpe and Use. Sometimes she travelled the twenty-odd miles by canoe, sometimes in the more comfortable launch provided by the Government, and at other times she allowed herself to be pushed in the little cart. Never before had she been so busy. In each of the villages there was a group of newly converted natives. They needed all the help she could give them to strengthen their faith and to help them to live true Christian lives. She was still fighting against twin murder, juju worship and the other native customs which were dying out all too slowly. Few were able to read. Women and girls were still treated as lower beings about whose welfare none need bother.

In the summer of 1913 occurred one of those red-

letter days which made up for all her hardships
and sacrifices. The work begun by her at Akpap
had continued to flourish after she had handed it
over to others. Eight years had passed and now a
fine new church was to be opened. Mary was
there, with her children, to be greeted by scores
who came from all parts of the area to see the
"White Mother" from whose lips they had first
heard of God's love and whose life among them
had won their confidence and devotion. Among
them was Ma Eme, sister of Chief Edem, whose
friendship had been such a help to Mary in the
early days. She was so deeply involved in heathenism that she had never professed faith in Christ,
although through her efforts many children had
been rescued from death. As the first service in the
new church was taking place, Mary's mind went
back to the early days, to her very first memory
of the place, to the time when she arrived to find
nearly everyone under the influence of drink and
lusting for blood. We can imagine how happy she
must have been to see so many of the people true
Christians and to know that the worst of the
wicked customs were things of the past.

Until the end of 1913 Nigeria was ruled by the
British Government as two separate countries,
Northern and Southern. The building of roads
and railways made speedy travel easier and at the
beginning of 1914 the two areas were united
under the Governor-Generalship of Lord Lugard.
This gentleman had heard of the wonderful work
which Mary had done among cannibals and

slave traders and he recommended King George
V to award her the Order of the Hospital of St.
John of Jerusalem. This is a high honour awarded
to Christians in recognition of service to mankind.
It was decided by the authorities that a special
ceremony must be held at which the award could
be bestowed. The official launch was sent to
bring Mary to Duke Town. The building in which
the ceremony took place was crowded to its
capacity. Mary was overcome with emotion. For
most of the ceremony she sat with her head buried
in her hands. When called upon to speak, she
found it difficult to say anything. At last words
came and she urged all who were present to follow
the Christ who had been her Saviour and Friend
for so long. She took little pleasure in all the
publicity she received. Like most great people,
she was truly humble and could not understand why she had been singled out for such
honour.

Back at Ikpe, Mary threw herself more keenly
than ever into the struggle against evil. The
native chiefs wanted schools where their people
could be taught to read and write, but they did
not want the customs of their ancestors changed.
This, of course, did not satisfy Mary. She insisted on preaching the Gospel and condemning
the evil practices of heathenism. When land was
offered for a school on condition that no attempt
would be made to teach Christianity, Mary would
refuse. Usually in the end the chiefs would give in
to the little old lady and Mary would then call

herself "the happiest and most grateful woman in the world."

The outbreak of war in 1914 caused her great anxiety. She feared that its effects would hinder the work in Calabar. She was due for another furlough and her health was again failing. At last she went down with fever. On January 10, 1915, she recovered sufficiently to conduct the usual Sunday services. Afterwards, however, she had a relapse. The doctor was fetched from Itu. For two days her life hung in the balance. Then, in the early hours of January 13, her tired body ceased to function and her soul went to be with the One whom she had loved so dearly, He who had first loved her and given Himself for her. She, in return, had given her life to Him. Her last words were in the language of the people for whose salvation she had toiled so nobly—*O Abasi, sana mi yok*. They mean, "O God, release me."

At almost unbelievable speed, the news spread that the White Queen had died. From villages far and near natives who had known her came to see her for the last time. The Government launch was sent from Duke Town to bear her remains down the river. A moving memorial service was held. The coffin, covered with a Union Jack, was carried by boys wearing black vests and loin cloths. She was buried in the land for which she had given nearly forty years of her life.

It remains for us to ask ourselves a question. What was the secret of Mary Slessor's success? How did this frail Scottish woman tame savage

tribes and persuade them to give up customs
which their people had followed for centuries?
The secret lay in the power of God. It was He
who had worked through her.

The key to her life was prayer. She called it
"the greatest power God has put into our hands."
She herself believed that she had been used more
than most because she had so many friends who
prayed for her. For many years she was working
alone, with no other person of her own race,
often no other Christian with whom to share her
deepest thoughts. Thus it was that she came to
pray more and more and to speak of Christ as
her Friend and Companion.

What of the work which she began? Did the
converts stand firm? Did others come forward to
take her place? What is Calabar like today?
I am sure you would like to know the answers
to these questions before you put this book
down.

At Arochuko, where Mary found the Long
Juju, connected so closely with violent bloodshed
and slavery, there stands the Slessor Memorial
Home. Here girls are trained in preparation for
marriage. They are taught to cook, to sew, to
wash their clothes, how to look after babies, to
keep poultry, to do gardening, as well as all the
normal subjects of a girls' school. Fifty years ago
they would have been fattened to become the
wives of chiefs. Older women are taught to read
the Bible and receive Christian instruction. The
missionaries who have been there during the past

forty years have seen many of Mary's hopes fulfilled.

Native custom still does not allow a widow or an unwanted wife to marry again. For such women, who are outcasts without any rights, much is being done. They are taught sewing and embroidery, using native designs which they copy in coloured silks on fine linen. Their work finds a ready sale in Britain.

One of the most outstanding converts to the Christian faith has been a woman called Nne Nne Mbafo. She was once the head wife of a chief who was the most important slave trader in connection with the Long Juju. When this man became a Christian, he gave up his many wives. Though he made provision for them, they became "outcasts." The head wife gave up her position in order to become an "outcast wife" herself. Thus she believed she could best help the others in that state. Her power in her heathen days had been very great. Even greater was the Christian influence which she exerted after her conversion. When twins were born or when a baby's mother died, she would bring the babies to her own home. Under her leadership, Christian native women built a home for these rescued children. In the course of the years the superstition regarding twins has slowly died out.

If today you were to visit the island where Mary Slessor saw the dreaded Long Juju, you would see little to remind you of the scenes of horror which took place during the lifetime of people still living.

At Asaga stands the Mary Slessor Memorial School where girls are trained to become teachers or nurses or in preparation for marriage. You should remember to pray for these girls who find it difficult to be Christians among people who are still following heathen practices. Men still have numerous wives. The old ways linger on in countless families. Much depends on these Christian girls if Christian family life is to be established in Calabar. There are similar schools at Ikot Obong and Duke Town, for this work is regarded as of first importance if the community is ever to become truly Christian.

The tribes are now crying out for education. They want to learn to read, for they believe that without education, they will never achieve wealth, power and success, which to them mean happiness. The schools are still run by Christian missions, though there are not so many missionaries in Calabar today as there were fifty years ago. Much of the teaching is done by native Christians, but some areas need workers from this land as much as ever.

The work which Mary Slessor began is going on. Today there are thousands of Christians in Calabar. But there are tens of thousands who have not yet responded to the Gospel, who are still enslaved by the devilish customs of their ancestors.

In the history of Africa Mary Slessor occupies a most important place. She had the vision of a great continent being brought out of heathen darkness into the light and liberty of the Gospel. Her own life she spent gladly in serving her Saviour. She accomplished much. In her footsteps have followed others, inspired by her example and zeal. They, too, have done much, but much remains to be done. She believed that the secret of all she did was prayer, not only her own prayers, but those of others who prayed for her. That is something we can all do.

> She climbed the steep ascent to heaven
>   Through peril, toil and pain;
> O God, to us may grace be given
>   To follow in her train.